Also by Robin Linke

BOOKS & PRODUCTS

The Little Book of Big Insights

Angel and Gemstone Guidance Cards

Happy Spray
(Energetically Charged Lemurian Angel Spray)

Visit www.RobinLinke.com for more information.

The Little Book of

BIGGER INSIGHTS

Angelically Channeled Messages to support a life of joy, abundance and ease.

Robin Linke

U¹⁰
You 10 Publishing

The Little Book of Bigger Insights
Angelically Channeled Messages to support a life of joy, abundance and ease.
Robin Linke

ISBN: 978-0-9848642-3-2

Copyright © 2014 Robin Linke. All Rights Reserved.

www.RobinLinke.com

Cover, book design and Wolf Logo by
Dichotomy Design
www.DichotomyDesign.com

Author Photograph: Mariel Pietrykoski

No part of this book may be reproduced, stored in or introduced into a retrieval system, or transmitted, in any form or by any means (electronic, mechanical, photocopying, recording or otherwise), without the prior written permission of the publisher and copyright owner. Without limiting those rights, the author and publisher grant limited sharing specifically of the Messages in your *public online posts* strictly under the provisions that you:

   a) Share no more than one (1) message per post.
   b) Provide clear attribution to Robin Linke on each and every post.
   c) Only use for noncommercial purposes. If you charge people to view your Web site or blog or want to use any of this content in any for-profit publication, you'll have to ask for explicit permission.
   d) Do not modify (make "derivatives"). Use only the entire message.

The author of this book does not dispense medical advice or prescribe the use of any technique as a form of treatment for physical, emotional, or medical problems without the advice of a physician, either directly or indirectly. The intent of the author is only to offer information of a general nature to help you in your question of emotional and spiritual well-being. In the event you use any of the information in this book for yourself, which is your constitutional right, the author and the publisher assume no responsibility for your actions.

You 10 Publishing

For my boys
Andrew and Christopher.
If not for you, I wouldn't be here today.
I love you!

Introduction

Welcome. Are you ready to talk to the angels…or at least listen to their suggestions? This book is a compilation of messages which I have channeled from the angels that are designed to support you in living a life of joy, abundance, and ease. If you are someone who has been working at communicating with the angels, this is a great place to start. If you already have a connection to the higher realms and would like to deepen your connection and communication, know that if you have been guided to this book, the messages included will be beneficial to you too.

Before we get started, I'd like to mention something about spiritual/energetic hygiene. Spiritual/energetic hygiene is making sure your energy field, your living space, and your work space are as clean and clear as possible. Everyone has a human energy field which interacts with other energy fields. You pick up on other people's energy and "stuff" all day long. Little bits of this "stuff" attaches to you and stays with you until you get rid of it. Have you ever been in a good mood, and then you run into someone who is in a bad mood your mood shifts? That's because some of their energetic goo has attached itself to your energy field. There are several ways to get rid of this. Cutting cords, smudging, sea salt baths, and meditation which I share more about later, are a few. You can also cleanse you and your space with my **Happy Spray** (Lemurian Angel Spray) which is available at www.robinlinke.com

Spiritual hygiene should be carried out daily. You should always begin and end your day with a quick prayer of protection. This purpose of this prayer is to help shine the light of your inner divinity brighter, thus keeping disharmonious energy out of your energy field. You can follow the prayer up with a quick spritz of **Happy Spray** or by lighting one leaf of sage and "bathing" in the smoke for a few seconds if you feel led. Just do something every day. If you're going through a difficult time, I highly suggest cleansing more often. Spiritual hygiene is so important to me, that I even used the word "should" many times… considering I don't believe in "shoulds", that should say something about it.

How To Use This Book:

There is no right or wrong way to use this book. You can choose from the suggestions below and see what resonates, or discover your own personal methods. Here are some of my suggestions:

I. With the book closed, ask in your heart or out loud what you need to know for the day. Open the book and read the first message your eye lands on.

II. If you have a specific question that you're looking for clarity on, keep the book closed, ask a question and open the book to see what insights it has to offer. Keep in mind that the insight may not be your answer, instead it may point you in the direction of the answer.

III. Read the book straight through.

IV. Choose to read one insight daily.

V. Pick one insight and meditate on it.

Angels and God

When I talk about angels, I'm referring to energies that are an aspect of Source, Creator, God, the Divine, the Universe (or insert the name of your Divinity here). They do not carry a religious connation for me. My way of working with God and the angels is very loose and open. I simply converse with them as I would anyone or anything else. If "Angels" or "God" does not resonate with you, replace those words with the name of the energy that does.

Grounding:

Grounding is a tool I use often, if not daily, to help co-create the life I desire. It helps you to be present and connected in the moment and with the earth plane. You can ground by sitting outside on the grass (or any other natural surface… boulders are awesome) and allowing yourself to fully take notice of how the ground feels beneath you. How it supports you. Be aware of the sights and sounds around you and find the beauty and peace of the moment. If you're able, lean against a tree while doing this. It will add to your experience. If you'd like to try a guided grounded meditation, you can find one for free at http://robinlinke.com/freebies.

Spiritual and Energetic Hygiene

Prayer

I highly suggest beginning and ending each day with prayer. Prayer consciously establishes your connection with divinity. For me, having that connection is essential to everyday living. I ask to be protected and guided throughout my day. Your prayer does not have to be flowery and pretty… sometimes all I do is literally say, "God and Angels, please protect and guide me throughout my day." Sometimes I use a more formal prayer. This is an example of one of my more formal prayers. Feel free to use it or adjust it in a way that resonates with you.

Dear God, Angels, Archangels, and beings of the Highest Love and Light, I ask that you surround and protect me and help me to shine my Light of Divinity in any and all situations. I ask that any and all guidance I receive bring joy and come from the Highest Truth and be for the Highest Good of All. I ask that I recognize the guidance and clearly understand it. And I ask that I have the resources available to act on the guidance with ease. Thank you. I love You.
And So It Is.

Use the same prayer before bed since you interact with others and receive messages during dream state.

Smudging

Of all the different kinds of sage (there are over 750 species worldwide), I prefer white sage for smudging. It's best to smudge with intent, so before lighting your sage, say a few words or a prayer asking for unwanted or unneeded energy to be released. You can smudge your living space, your belongings, your car, your energy field, your crystals and even your pets. White sage emits a lot of smoke, so it's recommended that you open a window in the area you are smudging, especially if you have lung issues. If that's the case, you can keep some sage with you in a small pouch as a form of protection against unwanted energies, or you can have someone else smudge your home while you are out. Another option is to purchase smudging spray (i.e. Happy Spray) and use that instead. Place a few leaves of white sage in an abalone shell, or any heat resistant container and light it. Let it flame for a few seconds and gently blow it out. You'll be left with white, purifying smoke. Walk around your space and fan the smoke knowing that all unneeded energies are being released. Once you're done, you can say a few words or prayer of gratitude if you like. That's it. Your space and you will feel a whole lot better.

Salt bath

Salt baths are a wonderful, relaxing, nurturing, simple way of cleansing your energy field. Drop a handful of sea salt into your tub as it's filling with warm water. Choose the type of sea salt that works for you. There's the sea salt you can purchase at the grocery store, there's Himalayan sea salt, dead sea salt and more. You can choose a coarse or fine grain. This is all a matter of personal taste. The bottom line is that it's the sea salt that cleanses your energy field. You can also include a handful of Epsom salts if you desire. This will act as an aide in the detoxification process. You can add a few drops of lavender essential oil for relaxation or some sweet orange essential oil for an uplifting energy. Or rose oil to bring in the energy of love. You may want to consider lighting some candles and putting on relaxing music to add to the atmosphere. Soak in the tub for at least 10 minutes. If you don't like baths, combine fine sea salt with honey to make a paste. Add a drop or two of essential oil if you want, and use it as a body scrub.

Relax and Release Meditation

Use this meditation to relax and let go of disharmonious energies.

Sit comfortably with your feet flat on the floor. Close your eyes and focus on your heart center… find something that you're grateful for. Let the feeling of gratitude fill your heart for a minute or two. Place the tip of your tongue against the roof of your mouth and let it rest there. Keeping your eyes closed, look up slightly and bring your attention to the space just behind the center of your forehead. Now, begin breathing deeply and slowly… inhale directly into your lower stomach. Keep breathing…

Breathe deep into your lower Belly and allow your body to begin to relax. Notice any areas of your body that are tense. Breathe into those areas knowing that you are breathing in the energy of peace and calm.

With each inhale, let your stomach expand… with each exhale, let your stomach contract. Take a moment or two and focus on your breathing. If any thoughts enter your mind, acknowledge them, and watch as they float away.

At this point, I'd like you to imagine that on each in-breath, you're inhaling pure, clean bright white light. As it enters your body, let it fill each and every cell, cleansing and soothing, gently washing away all your negative energy, energy that no longer serves you, your body, mind, and soul in the highest and best way.

Each out breath carries the unfavorable energies away to be cleansed by the Universe and reborn as joy and love.

Notice if there are any areas where you are still holding onto tension and breathe into it, flood it with light... envision the light pushing the tension, pain, and negativity out of your body, cells, and energy field. Keep breathing.

Next, you'll see a beautiful angel with a sword of light. This is Archangel Michael and he has come to cut away any energetic cords, hooks, or attachments that no longer serve you. Watch as he releases you from energetic burdens or habits that have been making you feel heavy.

Now that you've released those energies and filled your body with light, picture a beautiful rainbow of light over the top of your head, around your body, and energy field. Envision the colors washing over and through you completely. Allow it to fill you with sweet, pure, unconditional love... love from all that is.

When you're ready, bring your awareness back to your body and into the room. Feel the floor beneath your feet, notice any sounds around you, wiggle your fingers and toes... take one more deep breath in... exhale slowly... open your eyes.

(Record this meditation in your own voice and allow it guide you through the process.)

Cutting and removing energetic cords, hooks and attachments

An energetic cord forms no matter who we come in contact with. Everyone has their issues and problems, so once the cord forms, their problems become yours in a sense. Cutting cords does not mean that you're breaking off a relationship with someone or that you're not going to see them again, it's simply a way of releasing unnecessary energy. Energetic hooks and attachments are similar… have you ever felt like someone has had their hooks in you? It's simply a case of your energy being intertwined with someone else's and you don't need that. The easiest way to cut cords is to close your eyes and take a deep breath. Call on Archangel Michael and ask him to cut all cords, remove hooks, and release anything that has been attached to you and return them to God's light. Finish by asking to be filled and healed with white light and from God's unconditional love. That's it… easy breezy. Do it at least once a day… more on the days you feel drained. Or, do the Relax and Release Meditation included in this book.

The Angels and I hope you enjoy this book and find the guidance to be relevant and helpful. Thank you so much for taking the time to be here. We love you. We honor you. We appreciate you.

Much love and abundant blessings,

Robin and The Angels

Be grateful for everything you have in your life... the good and the bad. Remember, everything you judge as bad contains hidden treasures.

We're always in the background working to help you create your optimal life. However, we can't do much more than cheer you on unless you specifically ask us to help you. Even then, you may not recognize the events and experiences we are putting in your path that are specifically designed for you. We suggest you trust the experiences and trust that they are necessary for you to create what you desire. As we have said many times, we can come up with experiences that you may never have dreamed of. We can certainly create experiences you never thought possible. All you have to do is be open to receiving and accepting them.

Where are you feeling limited in your life right now? How can you change your point of view about that? What possibilities are you not seeing? Ask us to show them to you. Allow yourself to move outside your comfort zone and try something unfamiliar and uncomfortable.

4

Call on Archangel Michael today and ask him to cut energetic cords and to remove any psychic hooks that may be attached to you. This will help pave the way for more and light and joy to enter your heart and your life.

For those of you who have asked for change, yet continue to hang onto what no longer serves you, we have heard your request. We ask that you do your part and allow for the dissolution of these programs, habits, beliefs, relationships, etc. We cannot bring change to you with ease unless you make room and allow for ease in your process.

Today we send you blessings of peace. We ask that you look for the peaceful moments that are seemingly hidden throughout your day. They may appear as a beautiful cloud formation or as shadow cast by the sun. When you notice these peaceful moments let them to fill your soul.

We invite you to feel joy today. Joy is often forgotten while dealing with the details of the earthly plane. We suggest that you sing out loud, smile, and dance as though you were a child again. We realize that some of you may not have experienced joy even as a child. If that is your reality, then imagine what the energy of joy would feel like and embrace it!

With every thought that comes to mind and with each word you speak, we suggest that you stop and ask yourself if that thought and those words supports the reality you wish to create. If they do not, you may find it beneficial to cancel those thoughts or words and rephrase them in a way that actually does support the reality you wish to create.

Today we ask that you give yourself permission to follow your heart. For those of you who feel you are doing this already, take notice of your decisions and choices throughout the day. Are you really following your heart? Or are you choosing the path of least resistance?

If you don't know how to follow your heart, choose things that make you feel happy and light.

We ask that you remain clear and focused on all your intentions and goals. You may be asked to change a path or direction in the near future. Remember that not all goals can be reached by following a single straight line. If an alternate direction feels good to you, go for it. If it doesn't, ask us to show you another way. Don't forget to enjoy the journey for it is where you will learn your greatest lessons and obtain your greatest wisdom.

Did you know we like to chat with you? Sure, we're here to help and we love your prayers and gratitude but we also love to talk. Ok, so not everyone is at the point where we can have an actual conversation, but don't let that stop you. Tell us about your day. Point out a beautiful site, tell us what your pizza tastes like. Let's talk.

13

Today we ask that you connect with the energy of generosity. Many of you are generous of heart to others, but seem to forget to be generous with yourselves. It's okay to ask for help. You may even discover that many people have been waiting to help you, but didn't know how.

If you find yourself surrounded by too many people who are unwilling to lend you a hand once in a while, ask yourself what contribution they are to your life. If you are unable to clearly see their contribution, it may be time for you to rethink the connection…and yes, this applies to family members also.

15

Today we offer love and healing to any situations that are troubling you. Open your hearts to our unconditional love and healing. Let go of the pain and hurt. Know that you can hold onto the lessons learned without needing to re-experience the pain.

16

Welcome to this grand and glorious adventure you call life. When one sets out on an adventure, he/she meets it with curious eyes. Everything is new and exciting, even the experiences you'd rather not repeat. When you look back, you tend to laugh at the situations that caused you to learn your lessons. Imagine how different your life would look and feel if you were to view it and treat it as the adventure it truly is.

What's holding you back from taking inspired action? Today is the day to take one step... that's all, just one little tiny baby step towards one of your dreams. Don't get hung up on how many more steps you need to take in order to actualize your dream, celebrate the step you took.

How do you find a way to love a person you have been unable to forgive? Sometimes you simply have to accept that now is not the time for forgiveness. In cases like this, call on us to help with your continued healing. Ask to be shown how to release the pain with ease and grace. Ask us to send love or benevolent energies to your abuser*. There is a reason for their behavior and it is need of healing.

Abuse can come in the form of physical, mental, emotional, or spiritual.

Protecting your energy field is a necessary part of your daily life. You don't need to take on the energy of someone else's fear, bad day, or ill will. Some ways of protecting yourself are calling on Archangel Michael, surrounding yourself with white light, or expanding your light as far and wide as you can imagine. Carrying a black tourmaline crystal is another good option.

20

If you have aspects of yourself that you'd like to change, love them away. They have helped you to learn and grow. Hold these aspects close to your heart and have patience as you guide them like you would guide a child.

Are you open to receiving the gifts, magic, and miracles that the Universe has waiting for you? When you get stuck in the wrongness of life and everything that's not working for you, you close yourself off to the possibilities. You can even invite in more of what you don't want. Do your best to remain in gratitude and let the Universe know you are welcome to receiving the wonderful gifts it has for you.

Call on us when you are concerned about making a poor decision. Ask us to clearly point you in the direction that guides you toward your optimal option. The truth is no decision is wrong. One choice is simply more effective at creating and supporting a joyful life than the other.

Would you like to know what your spirit animal guide is? Meditate with the intent of being shown. If it doesn't show up while meditating, watch for what animals show up afterward, especially animals you don't often see or hear about. If you have an affinity for a specific animal, chances are it's one of your guides. You can have more than one spirit animal and different animals can show up at various times in your life.

When life's challenges arise, it's time to begin asking productive questions. Examples of productive questions are: "What lesson do I need to learn from this?" "Is there an easier way for me to learn it?" "What else is possible here?" "Can I change this?" "How can I change this?" The more productive and generative questions you ask, the more possibilities will be presented to you.

25

We suggest that you practice discernment on a regular basis. Whether you're giving or receiving information, take time to check in with yourself and ask if sharing the information is going to be helpful in some way. Is it going to help make another's decision easier, bring them peace, make them smile? If not, the information may best be left unsaid.

You are a member of many communities although you may not recognize it. You are a member of this community. You are part of a family, be it your birth family or soul family (including pets). You are part of the Universe which is an infinite community and you are part of the Angelic community. Remember these communities and call on one or all for support... even if it's simply for prayers and blessings.

27

Love is the highest vibration of all. Practice connecting to the energy of love on a regular basis. Doing so will make it easier for you to connect to this vibration when you feel threatened or are around upsetting people or situations.

When was the last time you gave or received a REAL hug? We're not talking about the quick hugs you give because social graces call for it. We're talking about a hug that says, "I'm glad we're sharing this space". If you don't have a person in your life you feel comfortable hugging with that much emotion, go to the pet store and hug a puppy or kitten. It can change your whole day and maybe heal an emotional wound or two.

29

Today we are reminding you of self love. It is the backbone of your existence. You must continue to find more ways of being kind and loving to yourself. It is truly the only way you will be able to fully give and serve in the way you desire.

30

Welcome to your new life! What are you going to create and manifest? A life of abundance and joy? Or sadness and worry? The choice is yours. Our suggestion is to consciously create from a place of joy and gratitude. It is that simple.

What energies are you aligning your vibration with? Look at your outside world. Who are the people you spend time with? Where do you play? How does your work make you feel? These are just some of the energies you are choosing to align with. Choose energies that make you feel joyous and expansive. Work at releasing the energies that feel tight and constricted.

32

When you get down to the bottom of it all, we (The Angels) and you want the same thing... a life filled with joy, abundance, and ease. This is our intention for you now and always.

We remind you today that sometimes things take time and require patience. If you find yourself getting frustrated or trying to rush things, take a moment and step away from the situation. Go for a walk, listen to music, meditate, read a book. Do something that will redirect your attention and energy for a bit so that you do not add the energy of frustration to your situation.

34

When you feel like you're riding the hamster wheel, never getting anywhere and feeling lost, it's time to have compassion for yourself. Remember that you're on a journey and sometimes getting lost is nothing more than a reminder of where you don't want to be. When you remember that you're doing the best you can and that your best changes moment by moment, you're more apt to find your way off the hamster wheel.

It's time to start being true to yourself and to let go of other people's standards. If you really want to change the world, begin by changing your relationship with yourself. YOU Matter.

36

When the burdens of life feel like they are just too much to handle, call on us to help you move through it. We can help you discover how to find solutions to the responsibilities you choose to keep and how to let go of that which is not yours to solve.

37

Spend some time meditating today. Create a fantasy world and play in it. Escape to the woods and connect with nature. These quiet moments create the space necessary for you to be able to deal with any stress you may be experiencing in your day to day life.

Sometimes when you take a leap of faith, you scream the whole way down. Now, did you take time to notice that you landed safely?

When you're feeling like no matter what you do, you're still not getting anywhere, move into the energy of celebration. Celebrate anything... celebrate today... celebrate the romance of life... celebrate your passions. The energy of celebration is the energy of joy and the energy of joy is never stagnant.

Who you are is determined by the size your heart. It is not determined by your job, your role, or what you own.

Are you truly grateful to those who have helped you along your way or are you actually feeling indebted to them? Gratitude has a flow of giving and receiving while indebtedness holds the energy of unworthiness.

When you follow the guidance of a teacher, healer, doctor, friend, or even God, that doesn't mean you get to relinquish responsibility for your choices or actions. You have chosen to follow (or not follow) the guidance. You may not always be responsible for the actions of others or circumstances which created the need to make the choices but you are always responsible for the choices you make, the actions you take, and for those you don't.

What if resistance is actually an awareness that taking the action you're resisting will create great change in your life? What would it take for you to be able to take the action and allow the change to unfold? You don't need to answer... just think about it the next time you feel yourself resisting and see if it results in any shifts for you.

Do you recognize the contribution you truly are? We do.

45

How many times has the Universe delivered what you asked for, but you turned it down because you didn't like the way it showed up? When that happens, rather than just saying no, ask for it to come in a different way with the understanding that you are limiting the ways in which you will be able to receive it... and may result in a longer wait.

46

Sometimes it's in the space of "not knowing" where we are open and able to receive the greatest gifts.

Raising your vibration is easy. It's holding the new vibration and keeping it there until it becomes second nature that can be challenging. Oh, and don't get too comfortable, because you're going to want to raise it more, and more, and even more. Just sayin'.

What if everything in life was a choice? What would you choose? What are you choosing now? What are you actually choosing now? Does your life align with what you believe you're choosing? Just something to ponder for today.

What creative and generative actions can you institute today to create a life of joy, abundance, and ease?

If a teaching doesn't resonate, look to see if it creates fear or resistance. If there is no fear or resistance and it still doesn't resonate, then it's probably not your Truth.

Did you know that you not only take on your parent's belief systems, your ancestor's belief systems, society's belief systems, but also the belief systems of your race, culture, and nationality? Beliefs related to culture and nationality seem to be the most deeply hidden ... and because most of these beliefs don't relate to your current lives, they are almost shocking when you discover them.

Have you considered the possibility that your body has its own consciousness and that it's consciousness may have different requirements and beliefs than your infinite self? What if you started asking your body what it requires to be in alignment with your infiniteness?

You are perfect at being you. There is no one else in the world or the Universe who has the exact same gifts and qualities as you. Why would you ever want to conform to someone else's idea of who you should be? Learn to live as the perfect being of love and light that you already are. Learn to love the aspects of yourself that you don't love. Ask to be shown how to heal the wounds that have created them.

54

We are here today to remind you that when you ask for our help, ask us to bring it with ease and grace, and in a way you will know, recognize, and clearly understand.

55

Our resources are infinite. Don't be afraid that you are asking for too much (or too little). It is our pleasure and honor to serve you.

When your family doesn't accept you as your true self, remember that it's their wounding and life experiences that have put them in a space where they are not vibrationally aligned with you. When you recognize that the difference is due to vibrational mis-alignment, it makes it easier to detach and not take things personally (even though it may feel personal).

57

If you didn't have something important to contribute to the world, you wouldn't still be here. You don't need to be cognizant of what you are contributing, just know that you are.

What would it take for you to be able to break resonance with the vibration of self sabotage? If you're not sure, call on the us for inspiration.

59

The definition of freedom while living in the physical world is the ability to choose without judgment of yourself or others.

Affirm the following: I am beautiful, blessed, and loved in totality now and throughout all my lifetimes and incarnations.

61

Pick someone that you'd like to forgive and ask us for help with releasing any pain, anger, resentment, or guilt you're holding onto with regard to that person.

When you hit those times in your life where you just want to give up, try slowing down and taking a break before letting it all go. Slowing down and taking a rest can generate a renewed perspective on things and actually give you the boost you require.

Be authentic with yourself by giving your heart and soul a voice. Speak your truth in strong yet loving way.

64

We're asking you to embrace the energy of joy, fun, and play today. You've been under too much pressure or way too busy to remember "play". Take a quick break to do something fun or to connect with a memory that brings a smile to your face and your soul. Give yourself permission to receive this gift today and let it soften your woes.

65

Worry only adds to energy of what you do not want to actualize. Is that really the energy you want to focus on?

66

Let your brilliance shine!

67

It's time to stop questioning the messages you receive from the Universe. We know that our answers may seem too simple or may not make sense at times, but you wouldn't be asking for help if your life was making sense.

Are you truly thinking positively or are you actually hiding from the truth? Positive thinking takes work, but taking it to the extreme where you're hiding from the truth can actually burn you out and create frustration.

69

It's easy to forget about the practical details of the physical life when you are focused on the Spiritual life. As long as you're on the earth plane, equal attention must be paid to both the physical and spiritual worlds.

Are you in vibrational alignment with what you're asking for? Limiting beliefs that are hiding in your subconscious could be the culprit for your request not showing up yet.

Receiving energy work plays an important part in navigating your world. Imprints from past experiences you may not even remember can be stuck in your cellular memory and create energetic blockages within your physical body or energetic being, creating fertile ground for more challenges in all levels of your life. Energy work helps these blockages to dissolve or move out.

Are you actually aware of what you are choosing? So many times we say we have no choice, but is that really true? What unconscious choices are you making? Be mindful of how many times you're actually making choices when you think you're not.

We'd like you to pay attention to your thoughts today and notice where your actions are in conflict with your desires. We'd also like you to look at your desires. Do some conflict with others? What can you do to bring them into alignment with one another and with you?

We are often puzzled by your human behavior. We see so many of you making yourself small. Why do you do that? It is our greatest wish for you to see yourself as we do. We see your absolute beauty and light. How can we not? You have been created from the same energy as us. The next time you begin to feel small or insignificant, please remember that we are all the same, we are all one, we are all The One.

75

Where is your life out of balance? Do spend too much time taking care of others and not yourself? Are you a workaholic who's forgotten what it feels like to have fun? Are you spending too much time focusing on the spiritual side of things and avoiding the physical? Balance is your natural state, when you take yourself out of balance and don't do anything to correct it, you're only setting yourself up for stress, worry, anger, lack in some area of your life and dis-ease. Why would you want to do that?

Have you considered deleting the word "but" from your vocabulary? Think about how you use it... it's almost always used in a way that impedes movement and closes off possibilities.

For every pain in your body, ask: What am I hiding here? Then be quiet and allow the awareness to show up in your life.

What if you just being you was what the world required in order to change?

It's really important not to take other people's judgments to heart. Their judgments are based on their life experiences and points of view. That doesn't mean they are True and you are not required to own them or accept them... unless you choose to.

If someone shares a point of view with you that opens you up to a new way of seeing things, awesome! That doesn't make the new point of view right or good, nor does it make it wrong or bad... It just makes it a different point of view... or maybe an interesting point of view.

81

Every time you choose something that causes you to feel constricted or heavy rather than choosing something that creates a feeling of lightness or expansiveness, you're limiting your capacity to receive.

Sometimes you just have to laugh and let the drama drift away.

83

Take 5 minutes today to put your feet up, close your eyes, and breathe deep.

Healing creates new and different possibilities, however, if you'd like your life to change, you must take new and different actions.

85

What would it take for today to be more fun, fulfilling, and magical than you've ever imagined possible? Don't try to answer the question... ask it and allow the surprises to show up.

When you look outside yourself for validation of your Truth... you're telling the Universe that you don't trust your Truth or yourself.

What if you were to actually BE in full and complete acceptance of yourself? Imagine what it would FEEL like. What if there isn't anything that you need to be that you aren't already?

88

Sometimes the only answer required is silence.

89

You have to be the most valuable person in your life and no one can give that to you other than you.

When connecting with your guides or any of the higher energies, remember that we NEVER speak poorly of you. We may be stern, we may be firm, we may be very straight-forward. We may even challenge you in order to get you to be realistic about your situation or your actions. However, we NEVER ever refer to you in ways that make you feel as though you are "less than". We NEVER call you stupid, or say you're unworthy, undeserving, not smart enough, not great enough, not creative enough or anything that even closely resonates with those energies.

91

Regrets are often the by-product of your expectations and how you think something should have turned out. Be aware of those expectations as you can never truly know what "could have happened" had you done something differently.

Sometimes we like to give you extra busy work. Why? Because it distracts you and lets us do what you asked without you getting in the way of your requests.

93

Dragonflies, like butterflies, are representative of transition and growth. If you see butterflies or dragonflies in an uncommon way, they may be bringing you the message that changes and new beginnings are on the way.

If you choose to do something that you feel obligated to do even though you'd rather not, be sure to off-set it with something that feeds your soul.

The earth does not require saving... it can and does what is required for it to survive. However, the earth does require love, gratitude, and respect. Take time daily to connect with the earth and thank it for all the gifts it freely provides, send it love, and respect it by recognizing when you are using more resources than you actually require.

We are here with you always... even if you don't feel us or recognize us, we are with you.

No one has the power to take away the truth of Who You Are... not even you.

You are Unique. No one can do things exactly as you do. You can share the same message as another person, even use the same words, and it will still be different. You're energies are different, your life experiences are different, your vibrations are different... therefore, your message will never be exactly the same as anyone else's. Embrace your Uniqueness.

What would you like to create? More money? Optimal health? A new job? A new piece of art? Whatever it is, be sure to spend some time focusing and working on it today. The energy that's present will fully support whatever you're creating.

When you're feeling overwhelmed or disconnected, go back to the basics. Take a few moments to breathe, pray, connect with nature, or focus on gratitude. Sometimes it's the simple things that are most effective in bringing you back to your center and reminding you of Who You Truly Are.

101

If you don't invest in yourself, who will?

Are you choosing for you or are you still choosing based on someone else's viewpoints. The times you are currently experiencing require you to be the Truth of Who You Are at Your Core and you can't be that person if you are ignoring your needs.

103

Your reality is as real as you believe it to be.

Sometimes, there are areas in your life where the only way to make a change is to Just Do It. You can call on us to help with any fears you may have, however, it's still up to you to take the action.

When you love you totally, you have so much more love to share.

When you deny your true gifts, you are robbing the world of the opportunity to receive your gifts.

How other people act is Their business...
how You REACT is Yours.

We are all connected, all part of the One, therefore, when you judge others, you are judging yourself. When you love others, you are loving yourself. Judge or love, which do you prefer?

If you don't take time to fill yourself with Divine love first, you won't be able to help those who need you as effectively.

What if you don't require healing? What if you're simply out of vibrational alignment with your soul? Take some time to connect with your soul and ask it what it requires so that you can be in alignment with it.

It's time to stop standing in the shadows of others. You don't need to aspire to be in the spotlight in front of the masses, however, when you let yourself be the Truth of who you really are, you're taken out of the shadows and placed in a light of your own... and... when you're standing in your own light, those who have incarnated specifically to join you on your path can now find you.

When you want to attract more playful and joyous energies invite the cherubs in. When the cherubs are around, it's hard not to smile.

If you want your life to change, you may have to embrace your inner weirdness once in a while.

When something is no longer working for you, rather than focusing on the pain, anger, and resentment, remember all the gifts you received before the energy shifted. It makes it much easier to let go without a lot of trauma and drama.

115

What makes you come alive? Do you remember? Do you make time for it? Spending time doing something just for fun is an important way of keeping your vibration up and your soul filled. You owe it to yourself so you can be the best possible version of you that you wish to be.

Having courage means you recognize your fears, however, you choose not to let them stop you. Pay attention to your inner guidance. If there is any actual danger involved, it will let you know.

You live in a free will universe. That means that no matter what messages or information you receive from Us, God, Source, Highest Light (etc)... it's your choice whether you follow Divine Direction or not. If God affords you the gift of Free Will, why would you not afford yourself that gift in regard to the limitations other people impose upon you?

When you are feeling stressed, consciously send your "stressed" energy into the earth... then consciously allow yourself to receive the pure, clean energy the earth returns to you. Don't forget to say a prayer of thanks before going about the rest of your day.

It's important to speak your Truth and choose what is right for you. However, this does not give you license to completely disregard another's feelings. Speak your Truth, Choose for You, and Do it in the Clearest and most Loving way you can. It's possible to be both loving and firm at the same time.

Change is inevitable. Do the best you can to breathe through it and ask us to show you how to make it fun and exciting instead of scary.

121

Sometimes you just have to slow down long enough to let things integrate.

If you don't use your tools, you're not going to be very successful at creating the changes that YOU desire.

123

If you want to thrive instead of simply survive, you must allow yourself to be flexible. Change is constant and if you can allow yourself the flexibility to bend and sway when the winds of change come your way, you'll discover more happiness than you could ever imagine.

124

Sometimes the optimal way to actualize your dreams and goals is by taking the long way around. Instead of getting frustrated over "how long it's taking", recognize and acknowledge the valuable lessons your learning and information you're receiving.

125

If you want to be at peace while living in the physical world, you need to at peace with your physical body.

What if instead of trying to "get rid of" your perceived short comings, you were to see them as a fearful child and love and embrace them instead? Do you think they'd remain as blocks to happiness or do you think they'd choose to vibrate at the energy of love? From our perspective, we see them choosing love.

The next time you feel down, look in the mirror and say the following until you start to feel lighter: I love myself even though I feel unlovable. I forgive myself even though I feel I have done the unforgivable. I accept myself even though I feel I am unacceptable. I trust myself even though I feel I am not trustworthy.

It's in the smallest things where you often receive life's greatest gifts.

129

Remaining in the present moment is the key to navigating life's challenges AND to appreciating it's rewards.

Connect with Spirit daily, how you connect doesn't matter... making the connection does.

It's important to hold your space and do what is right for you. However, it is just as important to communicate compassionately and respect those who are affected by your choices and actions.

The Universe always has more than enough to give, as a matter of fact, its resources are infinite. The question is, how much are you open and willing to receive? You're probably open to and willing to receive much less than you think.

133

Everything you desire is on the other side of your comfort zone.

You have everything you need to fulfill your destiny of greatness.

Do not allow fear to make your choices for you.

When you feel conflicted, it helps to speak about it out loud. If you don't feel comfortable speaking to someone you are close with, speak to us... out loud. Giving a voice to your thoughts and feelings helps release them from your body... however, there is a difference between voicing your feelings and complaining about them.

137

We love you... we know you forget it sometimes. That's okay, we'll continue to remind you.

If you truly want something to manifest it's essential to be grounded. Being grounded doesn't mean that you're unable to fly.

Are you just about at your breaking point? Congratulations! Instead of looking at it as a breakdown, see it as a breakthrough. Don't get us wrong, this takes practice. What is it that you are holding onto so tightly that is creating the situation? Is it stuff? Is it an idea? Is it a belief of the way things were/are supposed to be? Find that, experience whatever emotion it's bringing it up, and let it go... Keep practicing...

It's highly improbable that you'll ever be able to please everyone you come in contact with. Why not focus on doing what's pleasing and best for you so that you have the energy, drive, and desire to be of service to more people?

141

Don't confuse not liking the choices that are in front of you with having no choice at all.

Part of stepping into your magnificence is accepting your human-ness.

143

Did you know it's possible to use the energy of anger in a beneficial way? Instead of directing it towards things like re-living the situation that made you angry, or 'getting him/her back', use it help you create a change that is in your highest good.

144

Some days you are asked to make to a choice... and that choice is do you respect yourself enough to follow your heart?

145

Do you remember to ask God/Source/Universe/Angels (etc) for clarity when a situation is stressing you out? Ask that it come to you clearly in a way that you can understand and recognize... then remain open to receiving your answers throughout the day.

Find joy in the little things today. Allow yourself to be distracted for a moment and fully enjoy the gift the distraction has provided. You'd be surprised at how much those small moments of joy fill your soul and lighten your vibration.

Is there something pushing your buttons today? Our suggestion is to be thankful for the lesson you are being shown. Don't know what it is? Ask the Universe to show you gently and with grace. If that doesn't diffuse the negative emotions attached to it, ask the Universe to show you how.

Angels are God's administrative assistants.

149

Prayer: Thank you God, Goddess, Spirit, Universe, Divine for all the gifts you've given me. Some have been in the form of love and others in the form of lessons. I appreciate them all, am open to receiving them all, and accept them all... even if I don't always like them.

If you're not satisfied with your current reality, create a new one. How do you do that? Begin my making different choices. You don't even need to start with big choices, eat something different for breakfast. Take a different road to work. Put your left sock on first instead of the right. The more you practice choosing differently for yourself, the easier it will get.

Some days the greatest gift you can give yourself is that of silence. If you live with other people, go into a separate room or put headphones on to block outside noises. Do this for as long as you can. For some it will be only for 30 seconds, for others, it may be the entire day. Give your senses a rest and allow yourself to refuel.

152

Let go of your attachment to what you desire... set your intention and allow us to do your job.

153

We love you always in all ways.

154

Connect with the energy of confidence and let it infuse your entire being.

If you don't feel strong, ask us to infuse you with the energy of strength.

If you don't feel confident, ask us to infuse you with the energy of confidence.

157

If you don't feel competent, ask us to infuse you with the energy of competence.

If you are not feeling safe, ask us to protect you.

159

If you are not feeling loved, ask us to love you.

If you are not feeling beautiful, ask us to show you your brilliance and your beauty.

I reclaim the power required to make myself happy. I reclaim MY power to make myself happy. I no longer base my happiness on what others think of me. I no longer base my happiness on what others feel about me. And So It Is

The quality of your life is based on the quality of your foundation. The more you focus on healing, personal development, and strengthening your connection to God/Source/Angels, the stronger your foundation will be and the more satisfied you will be with your life.

163

To be enough, all I have to do is BE who I Truly am. To be enough, all I have to do is ACCEPT who I Truly am. To be enough, all I have to do is LOVE who I Truly am. I reclaim the power required to be, accept, and love who I Truly am. I reclaim My power to be, accept, and love who I Truly am.

If you don't acknowledge how you feel, the feeling will manifest in other areas of your life. Acknowledge your sadness, anger, fear, resentment, etc so that it can be released.

165

What is one small step you can take today that will take you closer to the life you desire? Why aren't you taking it? Everyone has at least one small step that they can actually take daily that will support the life they would like to create. Don't judge the size the of the step... if fear shows up, take the step anyway.

The only person who can make you wrong is you. Now why would you want to go and do that to yourself?

167

Take time today to quiet your mind and go within.

So many of you believe that you don't know who you are and in trying to discover who you are... you make things more complicated than they need to be. We know who you are. You Are LOVE. That's all you need to know, remember, and connect with. You Are LOVE. You Are LOVE. You Are LOVE. Look in the mirror, make eye contact with yourself and say, "I AM LOVE". Keep up with this exercise until you actually believe it.

16.9

Breaking a habit IS uncomfortable and it's rarely easy. Those are the simple facts. We will absolutely be there to help you, however, the uncomfortable part is just a side effect.

Did you know that when you always look for love and confirmation from sources outside of you, it could be more than a habit? It could be an addiction. From a healing perspective, it just means you need to go a little deeper to discover the source so that it could be let go and replaced with love from the Divine.

171

You are a powerful manifestor. Be especially mindful of your thoughts, wishes and prayers. Be very clear about what you would like to attract into your life and do the best you can to not focus on what you don't want or like. You may also notice that you're receiving strong energetic downloads over the next few days. If you're feeling uncomfortable in any way, connect to the earth and ask her to help you process the emotions or physical affects.

Your thoughts create your reality... but what if your reality doesn't match your conscious thoughts? That means, you have subconscious programs and beliefs running in the background that have more energy fueling them than what's happening in your conscious mind. Ask us to show you those subconscious programs so that you can release them and create something that's more aligned with your soul.

Connect with your higher self and ask it to speak with your inner child. Have it show your inner child that it is now safe for her/him to experience her/his Truth... and allow the judgments of the past to dissolve. If you're unsure of how to do this, let it play out in your imagination.

If you ask us for help, you need to slow down and quiet down long enough to hear or see our response.

Are you reacting from someone else's truth or your own?

Robin Linke is a soul healer and Angel channeler who helps people from all over the world to understand who they are and live life on their own terms by combining spiritual principles with practical actions. She is certified in a variety of healing modalities and the author of the bestselling book, "The Little Book of Big Insights".

Robin is an Advanced Thetahealing® Practitioner as well as being certified in Manifesting and Abundance and Rainbow Children. She is also a Reiki Master Teacher, Certified Angel Card Reader™, Angel and Tarot Card Reading instructor, Angelic IET® Master Instructor, Angelic Channel, Bestselling Author, Access Bars® Practitioner, Certified Dream Interpreter and Teacher, Hand Analysis Practitioner, Medium, creator of the Divine Core Healing Process, and the Angel and Gemstone Guidance Cards.

To purchase products and services,
please visit Robin's website at
www.RobinLinke.com

www.ingramcontent.com/pod-product-compliance
Lightning Source LLC
Chambersburg PA
CBHW061644040426
42446CB00010B/1563

PRAISE FOR ROBIN'S HEALING and READINGS

You give so much value in your readings and your guidance I appreciate all the time and energy you spend to help me You tell it how it is and give me courage to take the steps I need to take to accomplish what I want to achieve! Thank you for helping me along my journey. I know what I need to do, I will make progress because you made it clear when I do it I will receive everything that I want how I want it! Thank you! You are amazing! Thank You ~WD

I love you Robin! Your insight and clearing abilities have helped me so much in my life. God sent me a gift yesterday I've been asking for for three years! The Happiest day!! xo ~AB

You know, I have to say that if people don't know it or Realize it yet, you are the real deal. Your connection, intention, integrity and sincerity are all for the highest good. Robin, is a real true connection for our highest purpose, here on Earth. ~MR

Thank you …it's nice to know we have a place/and people to turn to when we let too much of this world in… ~anon

Robin is an amazing person and a Truly Gifted Soul. I have had the utmost Gift bestowed upon me by having a Soul Session with her. There are no words to describe my experience. But I can say that the Healing is Profound! On levels that have not reached me before now. She is a comfort to me .. and to my heart ~MB

A HUGE Thank you to Robin for a mind blowing clearing, dissolving, dissipating, Soul session yesterday …if you're OPEN to RECEIVE…Robin will make it happen. ~SS

Robin Linke provides a SAFE and LOVING environment for deep and lasting Healing to occur. I left my session feeling validated and supported – with new strategies and exercises to help me along the Way. Thank you, Robin (I slept like a baby, btw)! ~EF